Accidents of Birth

ACCIDENTS OF BIRTH

POEMS BY RICHARD LEIGH

Nettle Press
London
2007

© Copyright Richard Leigh 2007

Published by Nettle Press
jennifer.johnson@blueyonder.co.uk

ISBN-13 978-0-9533286-9-7

Printed in Great Britain by CPI Antony Rowe.

A number of these poems have been published, some in earlier versions, in the Nettle Press booklet *The Bellmaker*, in the anthologies *Poetry from the Spinning Room*, *The Iron Book of British Haiku* and *Iron Erotica*, by *Kater Murr's Press* and in the magazines *Babel*, *The David Jones Society Journal*, *The Honest Ulsterman*, *Improjazz*, *The New Welsh Review*, *Poetry London Newsletter*, *Poetry Nottingham*, *Poetry Salzburg*, *Presence* and *The Rialto*.

For permission to use the work on the cover, I am very grateful to Crown Point, publisher of the indispensable book 'John Cage Visual Art: To Sober and Quiet the Mind' by Kathan Brown. Thanks for permission are also due to the John Cage Trust.

*

by the way ...

CONTENTS

1
The Yiddish Word for Lambs   3
The Railway Children   4
Left Luggage   5
Untimely Thoughts   6
The Lampshade   7
Details   8
'The Property of a Gentleman'   11
The Vigil   12
Music Minus One   13
In the Armenian Church   14
Life Study   16

2
Gross National Products   21
Those in Darkness   22
Traveller's Tales   23
Mametz Wood   24
In Flanders Fields – the Movie   25
Martyrdom   26
The Leftover   27
Embers   28
The Bell-Maker   30
House, Drystone, Cathedral...   31
The Signallers   32
The Visitors   33

CONTENTS

They Will Take my Island   34
Ancestral Voices   36
In the crisp-packet...   37

3
A View of Rome   41
The Fayyum Portraits   42
On a Portrait, by Van Eyck   44
Turner   45
The Pencil of Nature   46
The Giacometti Room   47
Museum Piece   48
'As Seen on TV'   49

4
You Just Fight for Your Life   53
For John Stevens   54
Body and Soul   55
Two for Monk   56
Second Trombone   58
Imaginary Landscape   59
Mors Poetarum Conturbat Me   60
Epitaph for Lorine   61
Simone Weil   62
Stele   63
The Effigies   64

CONTENTS

5
Bayble Bay   69
The Herons   70
The Ships   71
Lyme Regis   72
Ocean   73

6
Coming from Evening Church   77
The Plough and the Song   78
Riga   79
'Votive Figures'   80
Photograph: The Poet's Childhood   81
Oh, I Do Like to Be...   82
The Underside   83
The Extra   84
The Poetry Workshop   85
The moon hangs...   86
Notes from the Cockroach Hospital   87
Inside the Chicken Centrifuge   88
Convocation   89
Nocturne   90
The Specialist   91
The dying carthorse...   92

CONTENTS

7

The Return of Ulysses   97
The Pillar of Salt   98
Lost Love   99
The Russian Lesson   100
Ask Me Now   101
...and in between times...   102
The Small Hours   103
Way out West   104
The water glows...   106
Landscape, with Saxophone   107
On Papa Westray   108
Orpheus, or the Power of Music   109

8

The Pyramid Builders   113
The Glassfields   114
In London Town   116
Ghetto   117
City Birdsong   118
Infection   119
Carcinoma   120
Endangered Species   121
In the Gardening Museum   122
The King   123
Lingua Franca   124
Widow's Walk   125

CONTENTS

Speed-Reading *Hiroshima*   126
Insomnia   127
Famine   128
Mounds of human heads...   129
The City and the Cranes   130
Ruysdael   135
The Hirelings, Melbourne   136
In this dawn landscape...   137
Montale Variation   138

Notes   140

For Sheila,
and in memory of Hrant Dink.

1

THE YIDDISH WORD FOR LAMBS

for Maisie

They can't help themselves
but be emblems of innocence

as they stare, so openly curious,
bright in the sunlit fields.

And I remember your name for them,
and for me, so many years ago, now –

'shepsela'. How often was it heard
in the darkness of Europe,

quiet as the last word of a lullaby?

THE RAILWAY CHILDREN

Scaled down, as if seen from far off,
the children's train chugs down the track,

the little elbows of its pistons working,
past model villages, and brightly-painted stations
at which it's always three o'clock.

The children have their brief encounters
with mothers and fathers and favourite uncles,

then clamber aboard the Kindertransport,
which huffs and puffs away. The time's
past three o'clock. Evening sets in, and rain.

The train grows smaller.

LEFT LUGGAGE

It is the smell of wood
that hits me first –
wood, and the damp.

Names on packing-cases
remind me of exile
and the irreversible loss
of towns and families –

their dreads, their fashions,
their transitory hopes,
revealed by the light
which filters down
on wirelesses
and standard lamps.

I lock the door behind me.

UNTIMELY THOUGHTS

There are still tombstones
somewhere, in an obscure suburb.
Of course, I need an interpreter,
a guide to the worn inscriptions.

I go back to the city.
In a bland new-town precinct
they have built a mother-wear store
on the site of the ghetto.

And as (I tell myself) we are all guilty,
I try not to judge these people
who handed back to the killers
two stick-figures for each sack of grain.

THE LAMPSHADE

**I never learned where it came from:
some department-store, probably,
blessed with regular consignments
from factories in far-off countries –
no questions asked.**

**I look back fondly:
cosy family gatherings,
a soft glow on the walls.**

DETAILS
for my mother

1.

I am in need of details to distract me –
look at the heavy clouds,
hope that the rain will hold off
until we are back in the prayer-hall.

I focus, needing detail to distract me,
on the smallness of the coffin –
this woman, so large a part of my life,
and how they economise on wood.

I listen to my voice as I stumble,
like a man dyslexic, through the *Kaddish*.

Against the sole of my shoe I can feel
the blade of the shovel as I drive it
clumsily into the thick clay –
the far-off impact, down there – a detail.

The old, as they move toward her grave
are moved toward their own – each visit here
further knocking the breath out of them.
One by one, the makers of my world
                              are leaving it.

2.

It had all been so rushed and clumsy:
a sudden lurch and thunder in the head,
and the tact of the ambulance-men,
and the nurse casting around for words of
                                          comfort,
and the incessant bleep of the life-support
supporting nothing, finally.

3.

Each time I return here, the cemetery
has pushed its boundaries
further toward the horizon.

We stand in the middle of a field
vast as an ocean in which your coffin
will bob like a lost boat, when we leave you.

Whiling away the time during prayers
in a language lost on me, I read the names
of the dead immigrant generations – Nussbaums,
Bialystocks, the rank and file of Cohens –
my people, or not, depending on my mood.
Right now, there's no-one close.

4.

I turn to leave, and think:
in a year's time, a pebble on your grave.
I think about Villon's Paris – wolves
tearing the dead from the ground;
and somewhere in Central Europe,
tombstones, the names eroded,
re-used as lintels and pavements.

Back in the prayer-hall, the children
shift from foot to foot, trying
not to think of something funny.

I listen to the eulogy – its facts in order,
the likeness wrong as a waxwork.

More prayers. With every year
there are fewer who can follow them.

I think about a woman in Africa, the last
to speak her language. What was in her mind
as she talked into the tape-recorder,
sending a relic of a dying past
into a future which wouldn't understand it?

'THE PROPERTY OF A GENTLEMAN'

in memory of Tony Burge

I sifted and bagged up
the maps, guidebooks, foreign coins,
the phrasebooks and stationery –
our single lives survived,
however briefly, by a skip-load of junk,
clothes to the charity-shop,
and then by nothing.

And of course it would be better
that your long self-willed life
could just have lasted and lasted,
the poems being endlessly improved,
your favourite books and cities
revisited forever.

And of course it would be better –
rather than thinking about your ashes
scattered in the 'dispersal area' –
to picture you sitting with Cavafy
at some eternal café-table piled
with the loose pages of your latest poems,
the two of you eyeing up the angels,
discussing your preferences and chances,
vowing to return at nightfall.

THE VIGIL

And now you stand at the bedside
or wander, distraught, the drab corridors,
their harsh light – the whole thing
almost held together by the tactful kindness
of those whose job it is to be kind.

You search for signs of recognition,
and the kind ones advise you:
'The sense of hearing is the last to go –
speak to him'; and you beg, command,
try to joke, remind him of family sayings,
awful aunts, disastrous holidays.

Your voice mingles with the soft
growling breath, as you watch
the random grimaces, the lips
drawn back in a snarl at nothing.

You thank the kind ones, and assure them
that they have been of comfort;
but this is now between the two of you.

A final sigh, and you call them back in –
they having just left you alone –
and break the news, and in your mind
begin to make arrangements.

MUSIC MINUS ONE

'He's looking better, climbs
the steep hill to the pub,
gets here only slightly breathless,
as well as he could be, really.'

For a few nights we miss the filthy laugh –
and then the news, and the funeral:
none of your friends, no-one who'll miss you,
no 'drunkards and musicians' –
only the guests your wife allows
to smother your memory with niceness.

But sometimes one of the drinkers
gets the next round in, orders
a pint too many. The barman
silently puts it right. The drinkers
briefly look at the floor.

IN THE ARMENIAN CHURCH

for Vrej

Before, I had thought about scalpels,
gauze, the glaring lights,
'sometime round now, it must be...'
and you lying there, so passive,
so 'at the mercy' - while I
had only the treadmill of thought
which couldn't resolve itself in prayer,
but just went on and on
until something stopped it.

Now, in the church, I can grasp
only part of the eulogy: the word for 'one'
referring, perhaps, to God,
or to the age of your son;
your name, repeatedly; a word
which might be 'gratitude', or 'grace'.

In the back row, a child,
confused and nervous –
I hope she wasn't close to you.
At that age, we feel personally let down:
the dead are holding out on us
for reasons we can't understand.

'It's not funny any more. Come home.
I know you're out there somewhere –
some mix-up at the hospital.'

Soon, there'll be the familiar sound
of his key turning in the door,
and then, an evening of wild talk,
catching up with the news,
trading reassurance and family jokes.
At bedtime, it's like Christmas Eve,
knowing that tomorrow there'll be more,
and more still, for the rest of our lives –

or almost: the details are vague,
and will have to be filled in later.
Later, we'll understand, or think we do.

But for the grown-ups, no such fantasies:
now, you are reduced to nothing
but an elegant pine box
piled high with lilies, carried
on the shoulders of six men
who can't believe what's happened.

LIFE-STUDY

The beach-towel, the picnic:
rain forecast, but delayed
until we were safely home.

Your selflessness:
small acts of kindness
as if by stealth.

Last week, you chatted
about television,
and the other patients,
praised nurses, flowers,
doctors and the weather,
told us your memories.

Now, we would keep you with us,
but there's no holding you.

Head, linen, feet –
stark you lie
in lessening state.

We search your mumblings:
does she still know us?

Medication timed to kill,
the body drags the mind
down to its rest.

Used wreaths, flung
in an old water-tank.

The distant relatives,
their garish cortège.

The earth a neat pile,
the grave a tidy slot.

2

GROSS NATIONAL PRODUCTS

A woman carries
the last of her starved children
to the communal grave.

Elsewhere, a woman
takes her dog
to the psychotherapist

and the headlines ask
'why do they hate us?'

and there's a sudden rush
on paperback Korans.

THOSE IN DARKNESS

Spin the globe,
point almost anywhere:

the same squalid agonies
in places known

only to experts,
until the headlines.

Even the best binoculars
useless from Parnassus.

An irrelevant expertise:
trainspotting at Auschwitz.

TRAVELLER'S TALES

You seem to have adopted that exotic land.
At parties and in pubs you tell us, endlessly,
about the dietary habits of its alligators,
the lazy natives, the corrupt officials,
the rain that falls each year for fifteen days
                                      precisely,
leaving as suddenly as it arrives.

You tell us – against our will, quite often –
about the fauna: the giant flying-beetles,
gunmetal-carapaced and poisonous,
and the shimmering wingspans of vast dragonflies
crossing unending swamps in the dawn light.
Somehow, behind the details you describe,
we can sense darkness, and imprisonment.
We learn of them from your tales; and yet it seems
you noticed nothing. We must picture for ourselves
what was before your eyes.
You mentioned a brothel concealed
beneath some office-block at the edge of town,
housing the standard erotic merchandise –
but did you sample it? You haven't told us.
You admitted fear; but only of the mess
of some malarial bowel-movement
which threatened, once, to inconvenience you.
When you tell your stories, it's as if
there had been dancing on the mass graves,
but all you can remember is the music.

MAMETZ WOOD

'Like landscape', you murmur
toward dawn, your fingertips
lightly tracing my spine;

and I think of the soldier
who hurls himself
into the shallowest
indentation of the *nullah*
praying that the shells
will pass by him.

As sleep reclaims me
I think of soldiers' postings
and of my holiday plans,

turn from others' memories
which haunt me, back
to what is now, and mine.

IN FLANDERS FIELDS – THE MOVIE

At first I think it's just the pace of the film –
quaint as photos in sepia, the way they would
                                jerk along;
but this boy was maimed in his first days of war,
flung like a doll from a pram: severe spinal
                                   trauma.

He twitches and drools, while the nurse mops up
and tries to wipe his face for him, and wants
to smile reassurance at this wreckage
that hurls itself from side to side in its wheelchair
and can't be still enough to look at her,
convulsed as he is in silent screaming.

He is so far beyond the reach of help
that pity overwhelms me but still feels
as if it were a kind of condescension.

My freedom to stare at him and not be seen,
nor be reproached because I come afterwards,
into an age of safety, makes me ashamed.

I wonder how the documentary-makers
might feel about their work of propaganda
designed to show that *something* was being done.
And his parents – invited to a private screening?

MARTYRDOM

After the cold Latin
the headsman brings his blade
smashing through bone and sinew.

A mist of red droplets hangs,
for an instant, on the air.

Let the funerals go quietly by
as if they were not your own.

THE LEFTOVER

He had been given the words:
government issue, soiled.

He had been given the rule-book:
cryptic, peremptory.

Now, through the rubble of his home town,
they made him march on his knees.

From his cell he could hear nothing
but the black noise of feet tramping.

They flung him a few more days of life,
then forced him, once more, to his knees.

EMBERS

Armies have crossed and recrossed
this scrap of ground –
farms and villages levelled,
farmhands turning the wreckage
back into the soil.

In our plundered museum
a chaos of images crumbles
as the building rots and collapses.

In the remains of our temple
a butterfly flickers
across an abandoned prayer-book.

There is a slow and savage
tearing to shreds of the sky
as warplanes vanish into the hills.

Cross-hatched squalls of rain
soak into our blackened gardens.

History's film runs faster, borders
whip-lashing through one another.

Now, we know by heart
these lakes and valleys;
but the day could come
when we will search
our memories in vain.

Our lives were to vanish
like water dissolved in water,
our speech gone, in the air,
not to be captured again.

We hid in the ruins, until
the ruins themselves were flattened,
the land itself unhoused.

Then we were led
to the blinding light of slaughter.

But embers await the breath:
and the thick black ink, clinging
to the solemn, yellowing weave,
conveys a mimed and private wisdom
to lips, to teeth and tongue –
the sluice of speech runs freely,
the smell of earth fresh at the roots.

THE BELL-MAKER

The maker of bells
testing for resonance
and carrying-power,
imagines unchanging landscape:

in his calculations
only the shifting winds,
the varying densities
of summer and autumn air.

Dream perspectives:
hills, angled walls
give back a reassuring music:
bell-sounds, hollowing the night.

HOUSE, DRYSTONE, CATHEDRAL

House, drystone, cathedral:
hard to set stone patiently on stone
during a stay of execution.

Song is so easily smothered
in the torrents of speech.
Words are hard work; and yet
a line, a phrase, a single word,
preserved in a grammarian's footnote,
patiently awaits the light.

It's as if the work were done in darkness,
mattering to a few now, a few later.
The dead crowd us, desperate
to have their stories told,
to be more, for a while,
than just a fluttering of the air.

Somewhere far off, meanwhile,
sound-fragments –
love-song, war-cry, lament –
balance on the knife-edge of silence.

House, drystone, cathedral:
we have all the time in the world,
until we have none.

THE SIGNALLERS

Always it seems they are trying
to tell us something:
forgiveness begged or granted,
clarification sought –
since even they can't know it all.

But when they try
to make themselves known to us
they fail, utterly: the sudden
creaking of furniture in the small hours,
or the shadow that might have been
the edge of a wing:
moments which feel
like swimming into the cold.

At most, we might sense
that we are being addressed,
even in desperation;
but there is no message.

THE VISITORS

Entering the room
(who let them in?)
they move blank heads
on stiff necks, nodding
round to each of us,
not meeting our eyes.

Somehow they stand
in everyone's way
then move around us
and among us.

From time to time
their heads turn
to one another
as if they shared a joke.

When they leave, the room
is carpeted with dust.

THEY WILL TAKE MY ISLAND

two poems for Arshile Gorky

1.

Uneasy, serious, you stand by your mother
clutching a few flowers, staring at the camera
as if you see through it into your future.
For the camera-man, a queue
of the uprooted poor, who try not to blink
at the sudden blaze of light,
try to look brave, as if there were hope.

The image will be brown on black, high-gloss:
you turn it to the light to see it more clearly.
In another world, I turn it to the light.

2.

Learning your family name
I know you for a survivor,
know that what you could tell me
would be like poetry translated:

uneasy glances across the gap,
a need for copious annotation,
and still no certainty of understanding.

So small a nation, now, yet so much music –
response, perhaps, to the connoisseur
who threads the song-bird's eyes on a wire.

ANCESTRAL VOICES

A stream of motes in the slant light
under the slope of the roof.
The framed sky, with its flock of clouds –
then, the sudden dust wreathing upward
as the hatbox of old photos hits the floor.

The voices, thick as *kneydlach,* don't say much:
they seem, at first, not too concerned
with my South English vowel sounds.
But then their words – not to me, but about me –
set up a bass-line of contempt.

They mutter, sullen in the dusty air,
in words as fragile as Etruscan,
the only ones which I can understand:
schlemyrl, schmuck, meshuggene...

**In the crisp-packet
a blue paper twist of salt:
the night sky, the stars.**

3

A VIEW OF ROME
(after Piranesi)

Monuments praise the forgotten
whose names alone are immortal.

The long shadows, stark
against crumbling masonry –

a futile massiveness
reduced to mere caprice,

as strutting little figures
vainly gesticulate,
striving to arrest

the slow lapse into decay.

THE FAYYUM PORTRAITS

It is the eyes that hold you
as soon as you enter the room:
the eyes, large not just with allure
but with an unappeasable longing
to be alive once more –
large, also, with that fatalism
which stares unwaveringly
through all the slaughter in the *Iliad*.

The eyes seem to reproach you:
'Help us. If you don't, no-one will'.
But all you can do is stare,
and walk on, and stare.

Here are young men
who might feature
in Cavafy's dreams.

Here is Hermione, teacher of grammar –
thoughtful, as if in prophecy.

Here might be two barmitzvah boys,
nervous and brazen as any;

and here a Proustian hostess,
in jewels and purple –
the slightest sadness
about the mouth.

In the distant past, funerals
seem to take place in silence:

you can't hear the crying,
or the scattering of earth,
or the sound of burning;

but you can just make out
the rites of leavetaking,
the slow gestures.

ON A PORTRAIT, BY VAN EYCK

Look – the mirror
bellying
on the far wall

and we
in this doorway
an instant,
forever.

TURNER

To hold
the world

with this frail
cluster of senses:

the sun hacks
a path of light,

the blackness
of the water

carved to
a radiating
glimmer.

Somewhere
are boats,

a harbour.

THE PENCIL OF NATURE

...the sunlight
dead as the dust it picks out
seems to stir
to a facsimile of life
in the corner of the yard
where a broom leans
waiting for the hands
of the gardener whose shadow
can just be glimpsed
at the edge of the frame
as he stands briefly
in the cool shade
and misses his chance
to be half-shown,
half-hidden, forever;
and the light
suspended in early morning,
glimmers, where nothing moves
to blur the long exposure...

THE GIACOMETTI ROOM

Spindled remnants
impaled on space

ingrown distance

they are the bars
of their cage –
frail caryatids,
barely able
to sustain the air

edges
without substance

a weightlessness
so intense
it casts a shadow

in their fixity of need
they stride
toward
their absence.

MUSEUM PIECE

We wander amid the mute
wreckage of former worlds.

A dusty gallery: gloom,
shelves of bygone molluscs.

Vague daguerrotypes, portraying
visions of ancient landscapes.

Bubbling continents, engulfed
by steam and slime.

The drift, ton by ton, of lava.

Over the tracks of their ancestors
glide slugs. Lizards unendingly

pause – an age-long lethargy, mirrored
on the retinae of flightless birds.

Memories are stored, like Pharoahs' wheat,
in bleached and graceful dendroids.

'AS SEEN ON TV'

Our lives, our century reduced
to the gesturings of faded entertainers
and some man who is first on the moon
and some other men playing football
and one of them kicks the ball into goal
with only seconds, apparently, to spare,
and on the screen bulldozers
make their slow belated progress
into the camp, where they shift and tumble
innumerable limbs, and some of the limbs
could even perhaps be alive,
and they too think it's all over
and for them too it is, now
as the screen wipes them away, replaces them
with a moment of dramatic tension
from some soap-opera, and the limbs,
though of course they are not shown again,
are seen, still.

4

YOU JUST FIGHT FOR YOUR LIFE

for Lester Young

The world is vast
uncaring architecture.

Approach, as if casually:
you might insinuate songs
previously undreamed
into a gap in the masonry.

Turn a corner, then another:
heavy-lidded eyes
picture the next escape,
and the next –
a life of tightropes –
no other way.

FOR JOHN STEVENS

After a well-meant eulogy
which tries to be specific
but almost reduces you
to everybody's virtues,
and after you've been rendered down
to a handful of ashes and bone-dust,
it is finally time to drink:
your local, a closed world of noise, and smoke,
and booze, and awkward humour.
'Til chucking-out time
it hasn't really happened:
this is a gig, no more. And you?
Stuck in the traffic somewhere,
cursing God and man.

Out in the night, though, the truth
makes itself known to us:
you have been indispensable,
but now we must learn to manage.

Funeral-rites are the start of a slow letting-go,
memory is salvage, or invention,

and bereavement a powerless fury.

BODY AND SOUL: COLEMAN HAWKINS
AT THE RAILWAY HOTEL

Breath painfully compelled
through the rattle and clank
of the mechanism
eventually gives out the ghost
of an enormous music:
flesh being found, just once more,
for the bones.

Family, lovers, friends
all long gone, now, and you
contrive a system of *sotto-voce*
hints, obliquities, borne on a sigh –
the room filled, wall to wall,
with near-audible absence.

Leaving the gig, it feels
as if we abandon you:
decline arriving
at its natural close,
exit without applause.

TWO FOR MONK

1. COMING ON THE HUDSON

It was as if those boats
                    became
becalmed –
                        slowly,
from hull to hull, those
                        boats
  preserved in glassy stillness –

specific fruit
             of this
      particular afternoon.

You glance
            from time to time

  your forehead pressed to the window –

out on that so slow
                      shifting –
easily, uneasily, easily

                around, around...

2. CHORDIALLY

Tentative;
but for each phrase
the keys just so,
as if the years don't pass
but stay where they are,
gathering weight.

Openings
on further openings;
a swiftly-glancing
recapitulation:
this box of tricks
again obliged to yield:

each block-chord
a darkening articulation:
each line saying
there's no such thing
as repetition, –
the music coming,
each time it's heard,
from somewhere deeper.

SECOND TROMBONE

Maybe somewhere you can still be heard,
on airshots from abandoned stations,
or on the cracked shellac,
an extra voice, fleshing out harmonies
under the scuffling surface:
music made one ancient afternoon
for an impresario who never paid you.

Otherwise, only a photograph,
jaggedly creased: a mass of scratchy lines
almost concealing you from recognition.

On the bass-drum a name
ornately lettered,
grandiloquently obscure.

IMAGINARY LANDSCAPE

for John Cage

It might just be possible, now,
to work out the location of heaven
by the sound of laughter.

Where the various angels stand,
and what they sing,
are determined by consulting
the random number tables of the Law,

or the scattering of stars
seen from an unaccustomed angle.

MORS POETARUM CONTURBAT ME

The question won't go away.
We ask it as children; later,
trying to seem grown-up,
we ask it only of ourselves.

Still later, we ask it again,
helpless as children:
the times between, we filled
with easier questions.

The loss is beyond explaining –
but perhaps the words
taken down again, repeated, varied,
set to the sound of another voice,

will help us to push back the night,
speak – sing, even –
when we feel the need.

EPITAPH FOR LORINE

Far off, by water
and flat land,
the years passing
without great changes

your voice steady,
placing poems
carefully
on the silence.

One day, busy
with something
or other, we heard:
you'd slipped away

quietly as you'd lived –
life so easily over,
as if it didn't matter.

No pomp funereal:
just sad word of mouth
your memorial.

SIMONE WEIL

Your body
a poor gaunt
splinter
skin taut
across the skull
eyes huge
with anxious guilt.

STELE

Their names alone
hold your wife and children
back from oblivion.

Their faces are worn down
by centuries of weather
to just the slightest
undulation on the stone.

THE EFFIGIES

Your eyes, rapt, stare
at the high roof.

Do you see through it
the slow drift of stars
in perpetual night?

Your widow is crying
in the dim light.

Her unbound hair
flows over your feet –
stone softening stone.

5

BAYBLE BAY

The trickle and rinse
of water dancing
from pebble to pebble

under a scud of cloud
calm sea
the colour of old glass.

THE HERONS
for Harry Gilonis

Limber, brown feet
touch down, leaving them
free to turn, and
reticulate speckle
patterns complicate
the packed sea,

the inlet: noise
of each agile wave
rising, falling,
each reach
reverberates
as spray cascades

and the ceaselessly
battered dark deep
waves swiftly rebound,

the air thickens with wings
(far-off boats
bob like woodshavings)

– the heron aloft now –
a speck riding the thin air.

THE SHIPS

Calm at last.:
preserved in bottles,
galleons, their timbers
worn, scored
like old school-desks,
lichened and barnacled.

Take a deep breath,
climb inside, stroll
among decks, cabins, rigging ,
even hoist yourself
up to the crow's-nest,
reach out, touch the glass sky.

Stamp on the deck: on a quiet day
you might hear a low sound
like cellos massed in unhurried unison -
so close, you can almost smell the rosin
lifting like clouds off the strings.

Outside, like the slow
downward flow
of old windows,
the glass reflects
nothing but darkness.

LYME REGIS

In the walled garden,
autumn:

        the tree,
its bronze circle
on the rectangular lawn;

and beyond it
the sea.

OCEAN

A bird flies over the silence
of tiny-steepled landscapes

the ocean far below dredging,
again, dredging, at bedrock.

Flecked shoals drift
from dark to deeper dark.

Battered islands
gull-small, in northern seas.

The ship: harsh creak of timbers
as wilderness opens on frozen wilderness.

Remnants of the crew
die at the rails, gasping for land.

A wreck's black rib-cage
breaks the rippling surface.

The slow flap of wings.

6

COMING FROM EVENING CHURCH

for Samuel Palmer

Low above folded hills
the moon hangs: you can almost feel
the weight of it in your hand.

Church, houses, haystacks
cluster in the darkness;
and the forms of the people
huddle close, as they move onward,
and pause, wrapped in the night,
trudging the footpath home.

The children walk in a trance of sleep,
the old are supported as they stumble –

and behind them all,
a tiny oblong of penned sheep
white against the hillside.

Everything framed by an arch of trees:
the past, as a place of safety.

THE PLOUGH AND THE SONG

in memory of Komitas

The past, as a place of safety.
Back home, there was a song for ploughing:
a complex and ancient ritual.
The plough and the song were one,
turning the earth of history.

Your voice is powerful, trained
for the spaces of church and field:
it catches at the microphone,
which can't contain it: a harshness,
a desperation at the edge of song.

Your life: from time to time
a candle's-worth of warmth,
quickly snuffed out.

Now, the music is torn from you,
church and home destroyed,
history erased – and your final task,
a victim of arbitrary mercy,
is to take home the terrible news.

RIGA

for my grandfather

To me, it's just a place
distant in time,
remote, almost, as Jupiter.

But when you spoke the name
there was a sheaf of memories behind it:
a tree, the corner of a street,
details of stores, town hall, synagogue.

The sheaf is long-scattered, now,
and photographs are only references,
malign parodies, offering but withholding.

Their slow decay, in my imagination,
speeds up: they curl, distort
and blacken in time's flame.

'VOTIVE FIGURES'

A child is called in to dinner
leaving her toys scattered.

The sun goes down
for three thousand years;

and then, the scholars,
their diagrams and theories,

their calibration
of the effects of chance,

and the toys are scattered again,
precisely, in the cold vitrines.

I try to see the figures
for what they are

or might have been,
and imagine a child

who comes back
to claim them.

PHOTOGRAPH – THE POET'S CHILDHOOD

for Osip Mandelstam

At that age we're all afraid:
so small, we feel the cold intensely
as it comes rushing out of nowhere.

Today was a bad day: as you sat
before the rustic back-cloth,
your posture sad and constrained,

your eyes reflected all the suffering
present and yet to come.

OH, I DO LIKE TO BE ...

In the lounge of the Sea View Hotel:
horse-brasses, Crime Club editions,
ancient *Lilliputs* and *Argosies*.

I stare through the rain-flecked window
at the Municipal Gardens,
the benches in loving memory.

Jailed by the rain I sit
condemned to Patience, the columns
forever not quite working out.
I think of others' games –
canasta, whist, gin-rummy –
the grown-ups' ways of killing time.

Along the muffled corridor
the radio distracts me briefly
with news of Malin, Cromarty,
of this year's politics and glamour,
the weird names of racehorses
and hopeless Scottish football teams –

then back to the dull horror,
the inhuman symmetries: it's as if
I figure in someone else's game.

THE UNDERSIDE

A long, damp afternoon,
and night promises nothing.
Somewhere, just out of sight,
there's a slow dance.
The dancers might be
in separate times, places.
Somehow, they move
as if to the one music –
pastel-pale, inaudible from here.
And when the music ends
we shall be just as we were.

There is just the chance
to play once more,
to climb back on the ostinato
as if you'd never been away.
But when you heave yourself,
gasping, back on board,
the dancers have vanished,
yielded their places, moved off
elsewhere, out of sight, yet again,
but further, this time.

The nerves dance on alone,
through the long, damp afternoon.

THE EXTRA

Count, recount the children:
always the reckoning omits just one
camera-shy, standing to one side.

Glimpsed in family albums
is one un-nameable figure.

Later, this person
will reappear, constantly,
in holiday snapshots:

café, family, church...
and, just at the edge, a hand,
or the shadow of a hand.

THE POETRY WORKSHOP

In the white room
a scalpel-cold
condescension
thinly masked
by niceness;
and I am returned
to childhood:
waking each day
to unaltered misery,
life slammed in my face.

These others know
the tricks of living,
its mystery,
its justification:
my enemies,
the unfaltering
self-assured;
and when I hear
their tones of knowingness,
their smug, corrosive
complicity,
my childhood cries,
too late,
for vengeance.

**The moon hangs
bright as a lychee
low above the trees**

**you are deeper dark
on dark – a space
between isolated cries.**

NOTES FROM THE COCKROACH HOSPITAL

Sometimes there may be no choice
but to expose the workings.

However careful the surgeon,
a viscid whiteness
spatters the operating table,
as the body opens
with a soft sucking noise.
Then, the hot-butter sensation
as the scalpel slices into
and within.

Later, waving feeble limbs,
the patient signals life, or dying.

In the cellar, an obsidian heap
of abandoned carapaces.

INSIDE THE CHICKEN CENTRIFUGE

Inside the chicken centrifuge,
sleet beating on the tin shack roof,

the Masters conclude
their complex and arcane
experiments,

pack
(thank God it's Friday)
their briefcases
and leave,

as yolk
and white
slide
down the walls.

CONVOCATION

Here the philosophers convene
for their eternal dinner-and-dance:
a row of pearls and beards
around a long oak table.

The longest-dead of all the sages
creaks to his feet, claws at the lectern,
collapses in a cloud of bone-dust.

The shadow of the waiter's ribcage
stripes the wall, as he complainingly
sweeps the Professor away.

The fiddle scratchily strikes up
as clacking couples grimly take the floor,
hell-bent on pleasure (in a certain sense).

NOCTURNE

The grotto: a cool rococo haunt
where Dresden shepherdesses
grab the mike and scat their way
through prehistoric torch-songs.

The chain-mailed apes
and their baboon-companions
play anglo-saxophone laments
for pedigree chums killed in gorilla-warfare

while Minos thrashes the slack skins,
waking the spectral echoes –
and in the ornamental pond
catfish are swaying in time to the music.

THE SPECIALIST

'The Doctor will see you now';
and you mention your more superficial ills,
trying to play down their interest.

The Doctor is rumoured to take home
the more unusually diseased organs
as playthings for his curious offspring;

and the cats in the neighbourhood
slink in and out at the tradesmen's entrance
with a smug and predatory air.

The Doctor is said to purloin
the more outré deformities –
even, exceptionally, a skull or so –

making, on holiday or at weekends,
painstakingly designed and crafted
carvings, of a lace-like delicacy;

and on the surrounding streets
the rush-hour sees you trying to make your way
through a thicket of phantom limbs.

The dying cart-horse
stands
like a chess-piece
alone
in the field –
motionless
but for the swish
of its tail
brushing the flies away.

7

THE RETURN OF ULYSSES

And so we boarded the ship that would take us –
me, and my few surviving followers –
to a land beyond the reach of the sun.

I was still driven (I told them)
by a passion to learn about the world,
and the worth of men, and their vices,
and not to squander the short time left to me.

I had seen her across the blood-soaked courtyard
and knew that I could no more play the figure
who for so long had been the hero of her dreams.

Behind her formulae of welcome, and her tributes
to my undiminished powers, I could detect
a different note, and dreamed of voyaging.

THE PILLAR OF SALT

Children were screaming
on the walls of the city –
my neighbour's children.

She had known she was dying,
asked me to look out for them,
see that they came to no harm.

Now the city was burning
and we ran from it,
though I had begged to stay.

He had plans
for a new life elsewhere;
but children were screaming
on the walls –
I had to turn.

LOST LOVE

Our small-talk, over and over
tearing the scab from the wound.

Sometimes our words and laughter
chime, as before – bitter echoes.

My mind pads round the cage
of a single unaskable question.

When you have gone, I am stunned
by the expected silence.

THE RUSSIAN LESSON

I try to give you the sounds
just as I hear them,
that you will always find
me in this language,
as if you drank water
from my cupped hands.

We say, and repeat,
the impossible sounds:
yaziek, Russki yaziek –
and as you stumble closer
I seem to begin hearing
my tongue in your mouth.

ASK ME NOW

Shadows reflect
echo and lengthen
as we walk always
another block or so
our pace adjusted
to outlast sundown
the sky dimming bronze
mirrored in tall buildings,
the river, its boats
nodding agreement,
a walk that leads us on
forever murmuring
in slow misterioso
as we begin to rhyme
sound answering sound
always beginning,
as dusk thickens around us,
our words and silences
making a gradual music
nodding in sleep
as we are folded in night.

AND IN BETWEEN TIMES ...

And in between times we would talk
about experiments in ultimate
climax 'with a strange device'

and the daft fantasies we'd find depicted,
in detail, with po-faced solemnity,
by writers of Victorian porn:

the Maid in overjoyed amazement
at the inhuman stamina of Master.

You mentioned the uselessness
of multi-speed vibrators –
their abrupt, unsubtle change of gear –
and your preference for the slow
motion of peach-skin across vulva;

and I would gladly have contrived
entire fruit-salads of lubricity
if that had been the way to keep you.

THE SMALL HOURS

The curve of your hip
a silhouette
against the thin curtains.

I hear night's landscape –
train-whistles,
the steady-drumming rain –

then turn back,
keep anxious guard
over your quiet breath,

your drowsy mumbling
trying to tell me your dreams
folded into mine.

WAY OUT WEST

Dust-cloud to dust-cloud
you move through a blur of days
stop at small towns which quietly
clench at the stranger,
move off again into identical landscapes,
the sun rising, setting, rising...

Lying on the sand, you stare at the night sky:
it seems that, just as your eyes opened,
a single star had gone out forever.

The smell of your last lover
acrid for days in your nostrils –
was it you who lay there?

Drawn by the sudden lushness of a valley
you drink from polluted water,
ride off again, into darkening fever...

Later, as you waken in the saddle,
the plain resonates with silence,
as if a hand were laid
across the strings of a guitar.

Don't think of looking back:
if you twist round, it will be your life
that turns to stare at you
whitening by the path.

One more town: you enter
along an avenue of silent watchers
featureless in the dusk.

Another stop – brief,
without comfort – and then,
the road vanishing beneath you,
you move through a blur of days...

**The water glows, metallic:
in the gathering dusk,
the bright white of swans.**

LANDSCAPE, WITH SAXOPHONE
(after Hobbema)

The young man, in formal attire,
hammering sapling-stakes into the ground,
pretends he hasn't seen me.

My saxophone makes flabby, blatting sounds
out on the avenue. There is a barn
not far away: playing against its wall
might make the noise a bit more musical,
or not. The church, further toward the horizon,
will bother me with its bells –
their ringing tattered by the breeze shifting –
as I try vainly to remember
all the trite intricacies of the tune.

Attending vaguely at the edge of vision
are two or three other people,
blank-faced, like extras in a nightmare.

My music sags, and falters.
It seems the lowering clouds,
like moth-eaten hangings,
deaden the acoustic.
Home, and the pinging walls
of my practice-room,
are miles away.
I pack my saxophone, and race the storm.

ON PAPA WESTRAY

The dream unsettled me.
I'd been on lookout duty –
a hard day, as always –
squalls, and the sun
glaring off the waves.

My eyes focussed painfully,
searching the patch of sea.
That's where they'll come from,
if ever – sometimes, I wonder.

I could make out the shadows
of Spaniards and Japanese –
I knew about these, in my dream –
looming over me where I crouched.
They held cameras, guidebooks,
souvenir teatowels –
these things, also, were known to me.

I looked down and saw,
in what had been home,
only stones, and a scatter of rain;
and all I could hear,
but for the far-off wash of the sea,
was silence.

ORPHEUS, OR THE POWER OF MUSIC

Like a scattering of fine gravel on your back,
the feeling of someone's absence.

Remembering that the dead walk soundlessly,
you climb, counting your steps, try not to think.

Maybe the gods have never thought much of
                                        your music,
and as a joke reward your performer's vanity

with a woman who, indistinct in the gloom,
looks just like yours, sets out as if to follow,

and then turns back, and leaves you.

8

THE PYRAMID BUILDERS

Sun glares on tackle
as blocks are jockeyed into place.

Thirst: the mind
hears water crash and tumble,
land in slabs of spray, while
walls might crack on the iron blue.

The architect:
feet hacked off,
shattered ankle-bones
rammed in the ground, blood
soaking the soil, while we,
innumerable, heave this rock
against the sky.

And the jewelled, bandaged death within.

THE GLASS-FIELDS

Our ancestors toiled in the glass-fields,
eyes clenched against the glaring
shatter of the gleanings, the land
baked to a stupefying shimmer.

Many a field-day ended in torment:
fingertips shredded, and the eyes
a mess of blood and splinters.

By day, the Masters slept in mirrors:
but in the night-ink blackness of the Rotunda
they cross-bred, by force, the captive life-forms,
surrounded by silent anguish.

Across endlessly heaving fossil beaches
the Masters would grope their way
toward that manicured and vacuous landscape,
bland nightmare of the afterlife.

You could just hear their victims:
skulls paper-thin, life tenuously held,
quietly let go, like light-bulb filaments.

Here, on the site of the Massacre,
pedestrian precincts.
Tourist-guides
say nothing of all this: it's as if
the world had been created
about a week ago.

As you leave the city
you might detect
broken shadows calling
to their dead companions:
the Masters, fluttering and bleating,
as a red glow muddies the sky.

IN LONDON TOWN

In this city impermanent as cloud-streets
it seems that dawn, above the garish
glow of the lights, is just the sun
shrugging itself into the sky;
and you can almost hear
the stars mutter 'and so?'
as they fade resentfully from view.

But tall, black roller-skaters slowly cavort
backward, down echoing arcades;
and see how the trees look glutted, after the rain,
how pigeons strut across immaculate lawns,
and peace descends on rows of sleeping chauffeurs
in sleek and genteel limousines,
while lady harpists in deserted restaurants
play to the gently curling sandwiches.

GHETTO

What holds in check
revenge on the city:
penthouse, sweatshop,
a palimpsest
of shameful memories?

Night and day are made one
by the random timers
in the streetlamps –
the birdsong a nervous
unending staccato.

Architecture as power:
the empty stare of glass,
the roads as wind tunnels,
and in the back streets,
rubble and puddled beer.

The world as real estate
stands in its own light;
and we are crammed
into the final doorless,
windowless room.

CITY BIRDSONG

Past midnight. Out on the street,
demented, incessant birdsong
taunting us from a universe not quite ours,
which crowds us on every side.

The harsh blaze of the street-lights
confuses the birds with false daybreak.

Once, I believed that in the dawn chorus
the birds told one another their dreams.

Now, I know better: it is their relief
that the true day has finally arrived.

INFECTION

1.

The body swaddled in foil,
the bearers move slowly.
Light gleams off their visors,
as they stand to attention
alone on the tarmac
under the cold glare
of the arc lights,
then move off again
with an uneasy, bubbling
rasp of breath.

2.

Speak for infection's victims:
their few good deeds,
their few good days.
Adopt the eagle's viewpoint:
a cold panorama – the agonies
in their various gardens.
Speak in the voice of infection:
the world a laboratory, each death
a message in a bottle.

CARCINOMA

I grow unstoppably inside you.
Sometimes there's a pause:
you may call it remission,
I call it getting my breath back,

and then we're off again. I live,
I batten on you: what feeds you
is nutriment to me: we are brothers,
after all, under the skin.

Sometimes a merciless bombardment
might set me back a little; but remember:
what harms me, harms you more –
 you do your precious self no favours.

I and my kind want only to remind you:
you and your kind encroach without limit.
Your curse is on the world; my curse
on you, is a striving for revenge

for the balance which you have tilted
irreversibly out of true. Now, I control
everything that must happen, and
I am going to keep things like this.

ENDANGERED SPECIES

You don't know you're the last:

for months, years,
you wander,
hopeless, horny,
assuming it's just your luck.

The teeth of the trap
leave you disfigured.

You don't know
there's nowhere, now.

You can't know
you're the last.

IN THE GARDENING MUSEUM

How many hot untroubled afternoons
are stored in the heft of iron and wood-grain,
the pale watercolours, their loving detail?

Outside, the elderly in the walled garden
stumble, their soft shoes catching
eroded edges of funeral slabs

'RP, died 1636, relict of DP' –
stoop or kneel in admiration
of beds and shrubs laid out
in orderly profusion

taste on the tongue
the sounds of Latin,
a rosary of ancient names,
another enclosure.

THE KING

The King, in a room which overflows
with warmth and brightness
and limitless wealth, seems
to be gloating over his hoard,

hugging himself,
even dancing across the floor,
from time to time almost
levitating, for sheer joy.

So why does the King withdraw
to a secret room? And why,
a huge ledger in front of him,
does he inscribe his thoughts
in an unbroken flow, the paper
quite black with grief?

LINGUA FRANCA

What we have need of now
is a new kind of blasphemy –

something to bring
that old retribution

thundering down on us once more.

We had just a few centuries
to revel in the uproar and rush

the crush of phonemes, the air
a cluster of sibilants –

the tongues' dance – until
that bleak time when,

inevitable as a glacier
a pall of white noise

smothered the worlds of speech.

WIDOW'S WALK

Rocks drenched by spray,
dangerous, down to the shore:

a boat, beached for good.

She climbs slowly, each year,
to repaint letters
erased by the salt air.

Later, wind and sea
will destroy the name, the boat.

SPEED-READING *HIROSHIMA*

'Let your eyes
slide
down the centre
of the page –
the words
to either side
get into the sense
of what you read.'

Leaning precariously
over the side
he reaches
for her hands
flailing in the water.

Grasping, he sees
flesh
slide off the bones
like gloves
as she falls back
into the boiling.

'You get the drift,
the bare bones of it.'

INSOMNIA
(after Mandelstam)

Insomnia. Homer. The taut sails.
I must have read half the *Catalogue of Ships* –
that caravan of cranes, that vast shoal
which long ago spread out over Greece.

Like a wedge of cranes bound for strange
                                        lands –
on the heads of kings, godly foam –
where are you sailing? And with no Helen,
what can Troy mean to you, men of Achaea?

The sea, Homer – all is moved by love.
To which of them shall I listen? Homer is silent.
The sea is black: that thunderous orator
breaks over my pillow, roaring.

FAMINE
(after Mandelstam)

What is to be done with the levelled plains,
with their unbelievable starvation?

We think the emptiness is theirs – but then,
on the edge of sleep, we see it is our own.

And everywhere the question:
where do they start, where do they end?

And crawling across them, isn't that he
whose name we howl in our sleep –
the Judas of generations yet unborn?

MOUNDS OF HUMAN HEADS
(after Mandelstam)

Mounds of human heads,
off into the distance –
I live among them,
and no-one sees me:

but in favourite books,
in children's games,
I shall arise,
to say that the sun is shining.

THE CITY AND THE CRANES

1.

Maps, which are forbidden,
show the land around the city
as a pallid *terra incognita*
spattered with unpronounceable names.
The very shape of our country
varies, from map to map.
Once, the city was small, streets
winding around quiet churches,
with the muffled sounds of factories
at the far ends of industrial roads.
Now, the city is vast.
Our language, related to no other,
keeps us in isolation; and we are landlocked.
Because there is no night
under the ceaseless light of the city,
it is quite common for people to collapse
after long wakefulness, and to sleep
where they have fallen. When they awake
they sometimes recount their dreams,
and we stop what we are doing,
listen with great care, longing
for evidence of another kind of life.
A few of the crazed wanderers on our streets
are rumoured to have travelled
and seen living landscapes.

Whether these people's reason was blasted
by the intolerable beauty of what they saw,
or whether they are mad for some other reason,
and have travelled nowhere, we can't tell:
questioning them is not permitted.

2.

What we most long for is landscape.
On the rare days when the air is clean
we go to the edge of the city and stare
toward the hills, their anthracite mass
set off by whiteness where mist
blends with snow, the peaks with cloud
pouring from them, far beyond our borders.
It is a peculiarity of these
that they have no physical existence;
but if we try to leave the city, we reach
a hillock, a low wall, a shallow ditch –
a point beyond which we cannot travel.
One of our greatest painters
has made an immense triptych
consisting of details of tree-bark.
We stand before it in the City Gallery
drinking in the textures of wood
as if we absorbed something sacred.

In our places of worship, also,
there are carvings of vegetation.
They show what could be ours
but which the city denies us.
We gaze with longing at these works
during long sermons exhorting us
to be grateful for what we have.

The priests are part of the apparatus of law.
Anyone who believes their nonsense
is regarded with pity, or contempt.
Sometimes a drunkard will repeat such rubbish.
Later, he may be found at the city's edge,
dead, and much disfigured.

The city has a place for executions.
It occupies Freedom Square, the city centre,
the better to act as an ever-present warning.
We are not permitted to watch:
it is thought more effective to let us imagine.
Each day, the killing area is cleaned:
no trace is left of the dead
except the anonymous record of their crimes.

The executions are timed to coincide
with the twenty-four gun salute to the Founders,
and with the bells of the Old Cathedral
and of all the City's churches – noises
so great as to overwhelm the city.

3.

There is one night of the year
on which we may walk in the Old City –
the city as it was before the Improvements.
It is as though we can see those who lived here:
the desperately poor, their houses clustering
along the banks of rivers which are now sewers,
or were always sewers but are now enclosed:
rivers whose very names have been erased.
Why does the destruction of the Old City
seem such a crime? Why do we mourn
the loss of those hovels, those alleys
running with refuse and ordure, those buildings
crammed into one another's shadow?
Of course, the very walls were made of memory –
of wars, of wizards, of injustices
and their revenges, of the kindly, the eccentric,
the murderous – and on our walks
we try to play back the old city.

4.

Over our building-sites tower the cranes.
Some of us believe that the cranes are gods,
allowing us to clamber about on them,
press buttons and issue instructions,
as if the decisions were ours to make.
Others have written that the cranes are slaves
who will soon be goaded beyond endurance.

What will be the form of their revenge?
The builders embedded in concrete?
The cranes hoisting them to hang in the wind
until they die of hunger and exposure?
What cranes, or mutations of cranes,
will haunt the builders' dreams?
Nightmares of cranes stalking the land
like wounded insects, headless, unstoppable.
Nightmares of rivets, girders, steel cages.
A driver in his cabin, his face
pressed to the glass as he screams warnings
to the people below whom he must destroy.

What will the rule of law be, under the Cranes?
Do they govern the city even now?

RUYSDAEL

The fishermen's floats
in loops and arcs
resting on silence

each boat a world,
the bird-song distant,
faint, in the dawn.

THE HIRELINGS, MELBOURNE

Impossible not to rejoice, standing so high,
nerve and bone cut by the winds.

We build for our masters;
but what we build for them

is nothing but glass and steel,
and won't outlast the Earth.

It was our gods who put the stars
where they have been forever,

hidden from us now by the glare of cities
which will stand for a while, then crumble.

And the gods will look down again,
and see their world revealed.

**In this dawn landscape
drawn with a twig and a cloud:
a single figure.**

MONTALE VARIATION

And if the world fell from me,
left me shaking like a lone
aspen-leaf in a blizzard,

nothing around but immensity,
all direction gone?

And if the world returned,
with a soft slap
to the soles of my feet?

If everything resumed its place
with an air of innocence?

And if I couldn't say a word?

NOTES

Dedication
Hrant Dink was a Turkish journalist who worked for truth and reconciliation between Turkey and Armenia. He was murdered by a Turkish "nationalist" on 19 January 2007.

page 31
The last two lines of this poem are taken from Joan Retallack's excellent book *MUSICAGE*.

page 34
The title is one of Breton's names for a painting by Gorky, whose real name was Manoug Vosdanik Adoyan. When he went to America he changed his name, to avoid being pitied as a 'poor Armenian'. For background, see Peter Balakian's *The Burning Tigris*.

page 46
The title is that of the book by William Henry Fox Talbot.

page 53
The title is that of the biography of Lester Young by Frank Bűchmann-Møller.

page 55
The Railway Hotel is a pub in West End Lane, West Hampstead, London. Coleman Hawkins played there on his last visit to England, in 1967.

page 70
Most of the words in this poem were shamelessly stolen from Harry Gilonis' 'Pibroch' (Morning Star Publications). And when will someone get around to issuing a collection of his work?

page 78
The title is of another of Breton's names for a painting by Gorky. Komitas was the great Armenian composer and musicologist. See Rita Kuyumjian: 'Archaeology of Madness – Komitas, Portrait of an Armenian Icon'.

page 80
Lilliput and *Argosy* were short-story magazines popular in the mid-20th century.

page 120
This poem was prompted by hearing Mario Petrucci read one on a similar theme. Mario's poem will appear in his forthcoming book 'i tulips'.